THE MOST AMAZING NFL STORIES OF ALL TIME

FOR KIDS!

LANDON DANKS

"Winning is not everything - but making the *effort* to win is."

VINCE LOMBARDI

TABLE OF CONTENTS

Run Jimmy Run!	15
Kurt's Cinderella story	17
The Rocky Horror show!	19
Teaching them how it's done	21
When you've got to go...	23
The New Orleans Miracle	25
Money to burn	27
A Hollywood ending!	29
The... Steagles?!	31
The 55 year draft	33
The helmet catch	35
Full of hot air!	37
Eating his words	39
A slice of bad luck!	41
The butt fumble	43
Steelers #1 Fan	45
The FBI, Brady and the missing jersey	47

The curse of Bobby Layne	49
Favre finds... Favre?!	51
Worth the wait	53
The name game	55
A show of faith	57
The Cowboy Falcon	59
Head rush	61
When the going gets tough...	63
The Wrestling Viking	65
Deflategate	67
Man of steel	69
Fan power	71
Making waves in the Super Bowl	73
The greatest game	75
Trivia	77
101 Facts about football!	79
A quick favor	81

Run Jimmy Run!

The NFL has seen some unbelievable touchdowns over the years, and one thing that is always sure to get NFL fans up out of their seats, is the excitement of a defensive interception that leads to a breakaway touchdown.

That was the case in 1964 when the Minnesota Vikings faced off against the San Francisco 49'ers. Vikings star defensive end Jim Marshall intercepted a loose ball from the 49'ers, and, seeing an open green field between him and the end zone, set off at a pace.

The noise from the crowd grew louder and louder as Marshall picked up speed, gliding across 66 yards of uninterrupted turf to the end zone, where he triumphantly turned to celebrate his fantastic feat of athleticism and skill with his Vikings teammates.

However, instead of being mobbed by joyful teammates and basking in the glow of a wonderful touchdown, Marshall was greeted by a sea of confused and angry faces as it slowly dawned on him what he had just done.

Marshall, intercepting the ball, had looked up and seen an open field between him and the end-zone but what he hadn't realized was that he was facing his team's own end-zone.

He'd run 66 yards in the wrong direction!

As he launched the ball in celebration, all he had actually done was give the 49'ers a safety and put all the pressure back on the Vikings. Luckily for Marshall, the Vikings went on to win the game 27-22.

Despite going on to have a great career in the NFL, the defensive end has never been able to run away from what happened on that day in 1964!

KURT'S CINDERELLA STORY

Kurt Warner made it to the NFL via the *unlikeliest* of routes.

Quarterback Warner played college football for Northern Iowa for three years as he chased his dream of starring in the NFL. Despite his successful college career, not one single NFL franchise decided he was worth drafting! In fact, Warner would go undrafted for 4 years!

During that time he had to balance playing in the Arena Football League with a job stacking shelves in a local grocery store!

It would have been easy for Warner to decide that his NFL dream was over at this point, but through hard work on the pitch and stacking shelves in his down-time, there would be yet another twist in the tale of Kurt Warner.

After one year as an undrafted free agent, Warner was picked up by the Green Bay Packers, his dream finally realized! Or was it?

Things were never straight forward for this aspiring NFL star and Green Bay decided he wasn't good enough, releasing him before the season had even started!

3 years of stacking shelves passed before Warner was finally signed full-time to an NFL roster.

During his first season as an NFL starting quarterback, Warner was unplayable and he miraculously led the St Louis Rams to a first Super Bowl championship, earning him league and Super Bowl MVP honors!

Kurt Warner never looked back from here and went on to lead the Rams to another Super Bowl just two years later, winning his second MVP award along the way. Later in his career he took the Arizona Cardinals to a Superbowl appearance.

Warner became the only undrafted player to lead a team to a Super Bowl win in his first season. He was also the first undrafted player to be named both NFL MVP and Super Bowl MVP.

Warner finished his career breaking a host of records and achieving everything he dreamed of despite a difficult start to his career, showing it's never too late to chase your dreams!

THE ROCKY HORROR SHOW!

Robert 'Rocky' Bleier had always dreamed of being drafted, but perhaps not in the way it ended up happening!

After a successful college career as a running back at the University of Notre Dame, Rocky was drafted by the Pittsburgh Steelers. So far so good!

But that very same year, Rocky was drafted for a second time in entirely different circumstances.

It was 1968 and the USA was drafting men into the army to help with the ongoing conflict in Vietnam. Sportsmen were not excluded from the draft so Rocky, who had just started playing in the NFL, was recruited into the US Army and sent off overseas.

Unfortunately for Rocky, he badly wounded his leg whilst on duty. This would be bad for any sportsman, but for a running back like Rocky, having strong legs was even more important!

On returning to the US, doctors said that things didn't look good at all. In fact, the doctors were adamant that Rocky would never play football again!

Rocky was made of tough stuff however, and he was determined to make it back into the NFL. For 2 long years he underwent rehab on his injury, and gradually got stronger, faster and fitter.

During that time, he tried to break into the Steelers team, but each time he fell agonizingly short of making the cut. Maybe the doctors were right?!

It wasn't 3 years after being drafted to the US army, and despite doctors' advice, that he was finally selected to the Steelers roster!

Through sheer hard work, determination, and a never say die attitude, Rocky was back in the NFL. He actually went on to have a great career, winning four Super Bowls with the Steelers in the 1970s!

Teaching Them How It's Done

Chances are that you or your parents will have heard of the 'Snowplow Game'.

The December 1982 'Snowplow Game' was a regular-season game between the Miami Dolphins and the New England Patriots.

The weather in New England at this time of year can often be below freezing with plenty of ice, snow and difficult conditions. And so it was on this day in 1982 when the Dolphins traveled north to take on the Patriots.

Heavy rain and freezing temperatures had caused the AstroTurf surface at the Patriots Schaefer Stadium to freeze, making conditions underfoot incredibly difficult. And if that wasn't hard enough to play football in, a snowstorm then swept in to make things worse!

With these extreme conditions showing no signs of letting up, an emergency rule was put in place allowing officials to call time-out for a snowplow to take onto the field and clear snow and ice from the yard markers when required.

Conditions were so bad that as the game approached the end of the 4th quarter the teams were still tied at 0-0. Just imagine being one of the freezing cold fans sitting watching a game with no points being scored!

But there was drama still to come. With the game heading towards a scoreless draw New England were given the chance to kick a field goal. Patriots head coach Ron Meyer controversially asked the snowplow operator to clear a spot for the Patriots Kicker which he duly did, New England kicked for three points and won the game 0-3, causing much anger from the Miami Dolphins who felt this was an unfair use of the snowplow.

The part of the story you may not know is that the Patriots kicker that day was a man called John Smith. Smith was a teacher from England who was signed by the Patriots at the age of 24, after writing to them and asking for a trial. Although only an amateur soccer player with no NFL experience, the Patriots must have seen something they liked and took a chance on him.

As well as kicking the decisive field goal in the infamous 'Snowplow Game', Smith went on to have a fantastic career, becoming the Patriots 2nd highest scoring player ever on his retirement in 1984, showing sometimes it's worth taking a 'punt' on an outsider!

WHEN YOU'VE GOT TO GO...

We've all had that feeling of being desperate to go to the bathroom...and having to go quickly. But how many of us can say that's happened to us in front of thousands of fans in a packed football stadium!?

Well, Patriots legendary linebacker Larry Izzo is one of those people. Izzo was signed by the Dolphins after going undrafted and ended his career with three Super Bowl wins with the New England Patriots, as well as three Pro Bowl appearances.

But there was one achievement that would 'trump' them all for Izzo.

As well as being one the leading special teams players of all time, Izzo was a likeable and hard-working player who would go above and beyond to help his team win. And in 2012 Izzo had the chance to prove just *how much* he was willing to sacrifice for the team.

In 2012 Larry Izzo found himself on the sidelines needing desperately to go to the bathroom for what we can politely refer to here as a 'number two'.

Being a dedicated team player, he knew he needed to be ready at all times to come on and help his team. So when natured called in the middle of game, Izzo took the unusual route of going for a 'number two' right there on the sideline!

Despite a packed stadium of thousands of fans, Izzo was able to do the deed without attracting any unwanted attention!

The coach of the Patriots at the time was the legendary Bill Belichick. You could be forgiven for thinking that he would perhaps not have taken too kindly to one of his players carrying out this act on the sideline of an NFL game.

But Belichick did in fact see the dedication it had taken from Izzo to put himself in that position, sacrificing his ego, and risking embarrassment so he could be ready for the team when needed! He was so impressed in fact that he awarded Izzo the game ball for his heroic feat of ninja pooping!

What's even funnier still, is that this 'achievement' is still listed on Larry Izzo's Wikipedia page under his career achievements section!

The New Orleans Miracle

New Orleans has long been famous for its world renowned music, food, and vibrant people.

But in 2005, disaster struck when Hurricane Katrina hit the City, devastating people's homes, families, and leaving a trail of destruction. It what was one of the worst natural disasters the United States of America has ever seen.

As the people of New Orleans went about piecing their lives back together, things often looked bleak and unhopeful.

But as is so often the case with sport, the New Orleans Saints were able to afford the city some brief respite during the 2009 season.

As if written in the stars, the New Orleans Saints - who had never been in a Super Bowl before - not only reached the showpiece event, but went on to win it too!

Quarter-back Drew Brees led them to a 31-17 victory over the heavily-fancied Indianapolis Colts.

And although the Saints would never claim to have fixed the problems in New Orleans, the Super Bowl win did offer the city a great moment of happiness - restoring some pride to the region.

It was also reported that many of the Saints players donated large sums of money and time to help rebuild the city, showing that American Football *truly is* the people's game.

Money to Burn

Jim Marshall (Yup - the same Jim Marshall who in Chapter 1 ran the wrong way to 'score' a touchdown) makes his second appearance of the book. This time with an *entirely different* story!

It has often been said that football players are paid so well that they have money to burn. In Jim Marshall's case this was entirely true!

During the off-season in 1971, the Minnesota Vikings star defensive end set off on a snowmobile expedition with a group that included teammate Paul Dickson.

The plan was to spend a few days traveling by snowmobile through the snow covered mountains between Montana and Wyoming.

However, just a few hours into the trip, disaster struck as a blizzard blew in and forced the group to separate. As the conditions became worse, the snowmobiles started to fail, and having no mechanics in the group, Marshall and his party were forced to carry on by foot in the deep snow and arctic conditions.

They battled ferocious snow storms and freezing temperatures before deciding they were going to have to try and set up camp for the night.

With little in the way of supplies with them, Marshall and his group had to make do with what they had. And Marshall, who luckily always carried a lot of cash on him, knew just what to do.

To keep warm he started burning his cash, giving them enough heat to melt a space in the snow, and stay warm before eventually gathering some bark from nearby trees to keep the fire going throughout the night.

The decision to burn his cash ultimately afforded him enough time to survive the night and be rescued in the morning.

So, next time someone says to you that football players have more money than sense, point them to the Jim Marshall story and tell them that it is not always the case!

A HOLLYWOOD ENDING!

Thomas Henderson was a first round draft pick for the Dallas Cowboys.

He played in three Super Bowls in his first four years in the NFL, helping Dallas win the Super Bowl in 1977 and earning himself Pro Bowl selection with 75 tackles, three interceptions, two sacks, and two recoveries in the game.

Winning the Super Bowl for the Cowboys must have been a huge sense of pride for the Texas native.

But, perhaps unfortunately for Henderson, it was his performances outside of football that would bring him the most attention!

Nicknamed Thomas 'Hollywood' Henderson for his fast living and party lifestyle, he would soon find out that skill and ability *without* dedication and a good work ethic, simply wasn't enough.

His career started to go downhill just two years after winning the Super Bowl as result of his partying and, after a falling out with the Cowboys, he signed for the San Francisco 49'ers - but he only played another 6 games before his career came to an early end.

There was another twist in the tale for 'Hollywood' Henderson though.

In 2000, the former NFL star won a staggering $28 million on the lottery.

He used the money to set up several charities and is now a lecturer helping young people avoid the same mistakes that he made.

It just goes to show that no matter where you are in life, there is always a chance of a Hollywood ending!

THE... STEAGLES?!

No doubt you have heard of the famous football franchises the Philadelphia Eagles and the Pittsburgh Steelers. But have you ever heard of the Steagles!?

The year was 1942 and the USA were sending men to Europe to fight for freedom in World War II. This meant that both the Eagles and the Steelers were left short on players, and so an idea was born. The two teams would combine, and for one season only, become the Steagles!

It seems crazy now to imagine these two teams joining! Imagine what it would mean for the players and the fans if this happened today? But in 1942, out of necessity, this crazy idea became a reality!

The Steagles divided home games between Philadelphia and Pittsburgh and practices were few and far between. After all, players in both cities were busy working in factories and shipyards to help America's war effort.

On the occasions when they did get to practice there was an even bigger issue - Eagles head coach Greasy Neale and Steelers head coach Walt Kiesling shared coaching duties and the pair didn't get on at all! In fact, they'd often be seen arguing and disagreeing on plays for the team.

Miraculously, and despite the craziness of it all, the Steagles got off to a flying start, winning their first two games. One was a 17-0 triumph over the Brooklyn Dodgers and the other a 28-14 win over the New York Giants.

Despite some heavy defeats the Steagles finished the season with a winning record - some achievement given the circumstances!

The following year, the Eagles went it alone reverting back to the Philadelphia Eagles.

The Pittsburgh Steelers had another go at merging with a team - joining with the Chicago Cardinals. However, they didn't win a single game and earned the nickname the Car-Pitts!

THE 55 YEAR DRAFT

In 1999, Norm Michael was reading a newspaper like he did every day of the week.

But this time, the 77-year-old retired business owner was about to get the shock of his life!

Michael had been a talented college football player, playing as a running back for Syracuse Orange. At the time, he had been labelled as the 'fastest running back to play for Syracuse'.

Despite having a ton of potential, Michael never set foot on a professional football field.

But things could (and should!) have been very different for Norm Michael.

In the 1944 NFL draft, he was selected in the 20th round by the Philadelphia Eagles.

However, the Eagles were not able to locate him as he was stationed at Maxwell Air Force base in Alabama, serving his country in World War II. Remember, this was a time before everybody had mobile phones!

What is even more bizarre is that Norm Michael never even knew he'd been drafted until sitting reading a newspaper 55 years later!

He was reading an article in the local newspaper about every Syracuse player that had been drafted to the NFL - and saw that he was one of them!

Imagine how you'd feel finding out you could have been a professional football player - 55 years too late!

THE HELMET CATCH

The NFL has seen its fair share of incredible catches and last minute drama since its creation in 1920, but one play that always sticks in people's minds is the 2008 'Helmet Catch'.

Quarterback Eli Manning had led the New York Giants to a Super Bowl showdown with Tom Brady's New England Patriots.

With just 2 minutes and 43 seconds left of the game, the Patriots were 14-10 ahead. New England were closing in on an undefeated season that would make them the greatest football team the world had ever seen.

With just over a minute on the clock, and needing a touchdown to win the game, the Giants found themselves in a 3rd and 5 situation. Manning received the football on his own 44-yard line, but a heavy rushing press from the Patriots put him under immediate pressure - if Manning lost the ball here the game would be over.

Somehow Manning was able to evade the on rushing Pats and give himself just enough time to launch a Hail Mary pass long down the field in the direction of wide receiver David Tyree.

As the ball went up and the crowd held their breath, Tyree, who was surrounded by the Pats defense, looked certain to be beaten to the ball. Somehow however, he managed to shift his feet and time his jump perfectly to meet the ball in the air.

Miraculously and against all the odds Tyree had caught the ball between three fingers and the top of his Helmet, managing to maintain control of the ball under intense pressure from the Patriots at such a crucial time in the game.

The miracle 'helmet catch' gave the Giants the perfect platform for Manning to find wide receiver Plaico Burress in the end-zone to secure a 17-14 Super Bowl victory and one of the biggest and most dramatic upsets in Super Bowl history.

David Tyree's quick thinking on such a crucial play just goes to show that when you're under pressure it's often best to just use your head!

FULL OF HOT AIR!

The Super Bowl is known around the world not only for being the greatest sporting event on the planet, but for having the greatest half-time show on Earth.

In 1969, on the way to Super Bowl IV, the Minnesota Vikings decided to try their hand at a half-time show with near disastrous consequences! The Minnesota Vikings were up against the San Francisco 49'ers at a snow covered Metropolitan stadium with a place in the Super Bowl against the Kansas City Chiefs on the line.

The game itself was largely unmemorable - it was the half-time show that would be remembered in football history, and for all the wrong reasons!

The genius half-time plan was to send a hot air balloon and its owner up into the air whilst whilst using a 200 ft rope to keep the balloon tethered to the field. The person riding it would then be pulled back down safely and securely.

However the Vikings half-time show didn't go to plan at all! Due to the extra weight of snow on the balloon it failed to lift off. And so with quick thinking the woman who owned the balloon jumped out and let her 11-year-old son and mascot for the day Rick Snyder jumped in. They were hoping that less weight in the balloon would see it rise.

It worked! The balloon started to rise into the air as planned. In fact, it rose so quickly that the rope securing it to the ground snapped!

11-year-old Snyder found himself flying solo in a hot air balloon as fans watched on open mouthed!

As he kept on rising, some of the crowd presumed it was all part of the show, but it most certainly was not! Local air traffic control even had to get involved as they halted planes from flying anywhere near the runaway balloon

After flying for an incredible three miles, Snyder was able to release some of the hot air from the balloon and bring himself down, landing with a bump and a splash into the freezing cold Minnesota River.

Snyder was able to swim to shore with nothing more than soggy snow boots, a few bruises and a legendary tale to tell his friends!

EATING HIS WORDS

In the NFL confidence is usually a good thing.

But sometimes overconfidence without the ability to back it up can be pretty embarrassing...

This was certainly the case for the Seattle Seahawks and their quarterback Matt Hasslebeck, who found out that words are meaningless if you can't back them up!

In 2004, during a fiercely contested first round play-off game against the Green Bay Packers, the game was tied at 27-27 and heading into overtime.

Hasslebeck went up for the coin toss and, on winning the toss, proclaimed a sentence that fans of the NFL will always remember:

"We want the ball and we're going to score!"

This is a pretty bizarre thing to say at any time in a game, but what followed in the next few minutes is what makes this a truly memorable NFL story.

With confidence clearly flowing through his veins, Hasslebeck got set to receive the football, positioned himself, caught and threw the football....straight to Green Bay cornerback Al Harris.

Harris returned the pick, running 52 yards and into the end-zone for a touchdown, sealing an overtime win for the Packers.

Talk about eating your words!

A SLICE OF BAD LUCK!

In 2010 Detroit Lions wide receiver Nate Burleson played arguably his best game for his team, catching six passes for 116-yards in a 27-20 victory over the Redskins.

To celebrate his role in the victory, Burleson decided to treat himself to some pizza. He would end up wishing he'd chosen something healthier instead!

The wide receiver, one of Detroit's key players that season, went to collect two pizzas on his way home from visiting a friend when disaster struck!

Moments after Burleson had put the pizzas into his car, he started to drive. With the pizzas perched on the passenger seat, and the smell of freshly cooked pizza filling his nostrils, Burleson was no doubt eager to get home and crack into the delicious cheese based treat he had just purchased.

But as he drove off, one of the pizza boxes began to slip, and fearing both a wasted dinner and a messy car, Burleson reached over in an attempt to secure the boxes

As he reached over he lost control of his vehicle and crashed into a barrier - breaking his arm in the process!

We imagine Nate Burleson's coach wasn't particularly impressed with his wide receiver injuring himself like that for a pizza!

But there was one silver crusted lining to this story - the company he had bought the pizza from decided to offer him free pizza for the rest of the year!

THE BUTT FUMBLE

Sometimes, when things aren't going your way, the world can have a habit of piling on more misery.

The New York Jets were struggling in the 2012 season and would end up with a 6-10 record, missing out on the playoffs.

In fact it had been a decade since they'd last had a divisional win, so the hard-out-of-luck Jets could have been forgiven for thinking things couldn't get much worse.

But as low points go, things were about to get a lot lower for the Jets and in particular their starting quarterback Mark Sanchez.

On the thanksgiving day game against the New England Patriots, Sanchez was about to do something that would be repeated over and over on every highlights show for years, and this moment would even end up with its own Wikipedia page!

On 1st and 10 from their own 30, Sanchez snapped the ball and tried to fake a throw. But his plan went horribly wrong, and the Patriots defense was immediately all over him.

Sensing he needed to do something to avoid losing yardage or being sacked, Sanchez sprang forward in an attempt to make up some yards. But he suddenly lost his footing and slid face-first right slap bang into the backside of his own right guard Brandion Moore.

Now like most guards, Brandon Moore was not a small man at all, and the sight of Sanchez colliding into his behind face-first is one of the funniest moments ever witnessed on an NFL field!

Steelers #1 Fan

Every NFL franchise likes to say its fans are the most dedicated and passionate supporters in the world. But one Steelers fan took the meaning of the word 'fanatic' to the extreme during Super Bowl XIII.

The Pittsburgh Steelers were facing off against the Dallas Cowboys in a hotly anticipated Super Bowl showdown. The game saw both sides exchanging scores in an exhilarating match-up. The 4th quarter alone saw 28 points scored before Pittsburgh ran out 35-31 winners and were crowned Super Bowl champions.

As the Steelers celebrated their glorious triumph, the victory party went from the pitch and into the changing rooms where the players shared drinks, danced, and got showered before carrying on the celebrations long into the night.

As the team celebrated, they were joined by reporters keen to capture the happy scenes unfolding before them, and maybe snag some interviews with some of the players. But one reporter who had been following the Steelers all season noticed something no one else had.

Perhaps it was the champagne that was spraying everywhere, or the craziness of all the celebrations, but somehow nobody from the Steelers had noticed the extra person who was now joining in the celebrations with them.

A Steelers fan, clearly caught up in all the excitement, had somehow made his way past security and got into the Steelers locker room. Not content with just watching the celebration unfold, he had posed as a player and even answered some questions about the game from reporters before stripping off and joining the players in the showers!

It was only when a reporter familiar with the Steelers players and staff noticed him that the fan was finally found out! He quickly got changed and left the party... never to be identified.

What a story to tell his grandchildren, although it's unlikely they would believe he's the unidentified naked party man!

THE FBI, BRADY AND THE MISSING JERSEY

Tom Brady is the most famous football player of the modern era, and probably of all time! It's safe to say that as a player he never went missing, however, you cannot say the same about his jersey!

The 2017 Super Bowl saw Brady's New England Patriots overcome Matt Ryan's Atlanta Falcons in a thrilling 34-28 win for New England. The game also saw the biggest comeback ever in a Super Bowl (but more about that later in the book!)

Brady could be forgiven for being distracted, given he'd just led the Patriots to a famous Super Bowl victory *and* was the most in demand player in the stadium.

However, after the game, Brady noticed that his match winning jersey had somehow gone missing! Clearly that jersey would have had huge sentimental value for Brady and would have been worth quite a lot of money as well!

Brady reported the jersey stolen, and not before long, the FBI were involved in an investigation into finding the missing jersey.

The FBI, being incredibly good at finding things, soon located the jersey alongside another 'lost' Brady jersey from a previous Super Bowl. They were at the home of a news reporter who had taken the jerseys home.

The jerseys were returned to a very thankful Brady who, as far as we know, has never lost another jersey since!

Imagine how useful it would be if you could call on the help of the FBI every time you lost something!

THE CURSE OF BOBBY LAYNE

The curse of Bobby Layne is part of NFL folklore.

It is an urban legend that dates back to 1958, and it refers to a disgruntled Detroit Lions player putting a curse on the team to stop them being successful on the field.

Bobby Layne was the star quarterback of a Detroit Lions team that had won three NFC championships, but the year after leading them to their third championship win, Layne was inexplicably traded to Pittsburgh! A furious Layne is reported to have said;

"This team will not win another (championship) for 50 years!"

Following the Bobby Layne curse, the Detroit Lions would have to wait another 34 years before recording a playoff win, finally breaking the 'curse' in the 1991 season when they beat the Dallas Cowboys 38-6.

Or so they thought...it wasn't until 2023 that the Lions would win another playoff game, beating the LA Rams 24-23 and finally ending the longest winless post-season drought in NFL history!

In fact the down on their luck Detroit Lions are the only franchise operational for the entirety of the Super Bowl era (1967- present day) to not appear in the Super Bowl!

And with only one playoff win over 66 years and with two separate stretches of 30 years without a playoff win, the hapless Lions also hold the not-so-proud record of the league's longest postseason win drought!

Whether you believe in the curse of Bobby Layne or not, you have to admit there sure is something spooky going on with the Detroit Lions to be that unlucky!?

Favre Finds... Favre?!

Brett Favre had a long and established career in the NFL, playing for 20 seasons and making a staggering 321 consecutive starts from 1992 to 2010, including 297 regular season games, a record in the NFL!

Most of Favre's appearances came over 16 seasons as quarterback for the Green Bay Packers. In this time he helped them to 11 playoff appearances, seven division titles, and four NFC Championship Games. If that wasn't enough he also steered the Packers to two consecutive Super Bowl appearances, including a Super Bowl win in the 1996-1997 season - breaking a Packers drought that had stretched nearly three decades.

But things weren't always so straight forward for the Packers star quarterback. In fact if you were sat watching Brett Favre make his debut for Green Bay in his first ever game in the NFL back in 1992, you would have witnessed one of the strangest debuts a player has ever made in the NFL.

Favre, starting as a quarterback for his very first NFL game, was keen to cement his role as the Packers number one quarterback choice. And he certainly made an impression!

Favre, clearly deciding he should throw the ball to a receiver he trusted, managed, somehow, to throw his very first completed pass in the NFL to...himself! You heard that right. The first player to catch an NFL pass from Brett Favre was Brett Favre!

Setting himself to launch his first pass of the football for his new team, Favre was put under pressure by the Tampa Bay defence, and as the ball left his hand the pass collided straight into a Tampa Bay helmet and right back into Favre's grateful grasp for a 7-yard loss.

It even happened again to Favre toward the end of his career whilst playing for the Minnesota Vikings in 2009 for a loss of 2-yards!

It just goes to show, sometimes you've got to take a few steps back before you can go forward!

WORTH THE WAIT

You have probably not spent much time thinking about what you would buy your great-great-great-great grandchildren for their birthdays.

But if you're a Green Bay Packers fan and want your descendants to have the pleasure of a season ticket, then you better start thinking about it now!

In what can only be described as a huge testament to the dedication of the Packers fan base, season tickets to watch them at Lambeau Field currently have a waiting list that stretches for well over 1,000 years!

Just let that sink in for a moment...if you were to apply for a Packers season ticket today, you wouldn't get your hands on them for over a millennium!

And it's not like the Lambeau Field stadium is small either, with a capacity exceeding 81,000 supporters! Which is not bad for a team whose last Super Bowl championship win was over a decade ago!

Those supporters who already have season tickets must feel like they've won a golden ticket!

The Name Game

The NFL draft is a huge day in the football world, with teams painstakingly plotting for all sorts of scenarios and outcomes as each franchise jostles for position to try and bag the next big football stars.

Draft picks are swapped, players traded, and phone lines around the nation go berserk as players are drafted.

So it's no surprise then, that against a backdrop of such manic activity and extreme pressure, mistakes can be made.

During the 2011 draft two talented players had caught the eye of several NFL scouts.

Jordan Cameron, a tight end out of the University of California and Cameron Jordan, a defensive end at California were both stars of college football and seemed destined for the NFL.

One team in particular, the Cleveland Browns, were keen on securing the services of Jordan Cameron, and as the clock ticked down on their pick, they called him to let him know the good news - he was going to be a Cleveland Browns player! The conversation that followed went something like this;

"Hi Jordan, this is the Cleveland Browns calling to tell you we've picked you to come play football for us, congratulations!"

"Uhh, thanks but the New Orlean Saints have already picked me..."

An awkward silence probably followed before he added..

"This is Cameron Jordan...I think you're after Jordan Cameron, that's not me!"

The Browns must have been incredibly embarrassed at the mix up, but the story has a happy ending, with Cleveland eventually getting hold of their man and both players making their moves to the NFL!

A SHOW OF FAITH

Many of us dream of playing football in the NFL. From young children to grown adults, the thought of pulling on our team's colors and running out onto the football field in front of thousands of adoring fans is something we can only fantasize about.

But for one player, that dream became a reality that he didn't have any interest in!

Eli Herring was an extremely talented college football player, playing as an offensive tackle for Brigham Young University. Herring's ability was such that a number of NFL teams had been to see him play ahead of the 1995 draft.

As a devout Christian man, Herring decided that he could not play football in the NFL as they played games on Sundays, which in Christianity is a holy day of rest.

He made his intention clear to all NFL teams that he would not want to play even if he was drafted.

The Oakland Raiders had other ideas though, and decided to pick Manning in the 6th round of the 1995 draft. Not wanting to take no for an answer, the Raiders were so keen to secure their man that they sent a representative to his house and offered him a three-year contract worth $1.5 million.

Manning's faith however was not for sale and he turned the Raiders down saying:

"Not that I would not have liked to have been in the NFL, but Sunday is a church day,"

Before adding…

"although a couple hundred thousand dollars sure would have been nice."

THE COWBOY FALCON

These days the NFL draft is a huge event. Millions of football fans around the world obsess over it in the hope that their team will secure the players needed to propel them to a Super Bowl championship.

In fact, the draft is so important that viewing figures far exceed those of some actual games of other sports like baseball and basketball!

With the increasing importance of the draft, and its huge global popularity, it has been streamlined over the years into just seven rounds of picks, making it more manageable for teams and more friendly for TV audiences too!

But back in 1972 there were a whopping 17 rounds meaning that as the draft went on, there were fewer and fewer chances of worthwhile picks.

A huge movie star of the time was John Wayne. He had been among the top box-office draws in Hollywood for three decades, and had a reputation for playing rough and tough cowboys and soldiers in films.

As the 1972 draft went into the 17th round, and with slim pickings available, the Atlanta Falcons decided to opt for an altogether different draft tactic...

With the clock ticking down on their pick, Falcons head coach Norm Van Brocklin loudly proclaimed "Do we want the roughest, toughest guy in the draft!? Atlanta picks John Wayne of Fort Apache State!"

The modern day equivalent would be an NFL team trying to draft Vin Diesel or The Rock!

We don't know what John Wayne made of being drafted by the Falcons, but the actor, famous for playing horse riding cowboys, would certainly have looked great galloping out onto an NFL field!

The Super Bowl is a career highlight for the football players lucky enough to play in one. The chance to follow in the footsteps of football greats, lift the Vince Lombardi Trophy and don a glittering championship ring is the pinnacle of the game. In football terms it just doesn't get bigger.

So spare a thought for Broncos running back Terrell Davis whose dream of playing in a Super Bowl quickly turned into a nightmare during Super Bowl XXXII against the Green Bay Packers.

Davis had suffered with painful migraines since childhood but had been able to manage them through medication, enabling him to keep them at bay so he could play football. It was incredibly important that Davis took his migraine medication, as without it he would be in a lot of pain and potentially start losing his vision too.

Davis, who always took his medication during the pre-match meal before games, for some reason forgot to do so on this day - ahead of the biggest game of his life!

Perhaps it was the excitement of playing in the Super Bowl or perhaps his routine had been disturbed by the magnitude of the day, but for whatever reason, Davis missed taking his medication.

Davis didn't notice he'd forgotten to take it until a collision early in the game suddenly brought on a migraine. His head started pounding and his vision became blurred but his coach wanted to keep him on the pitch as a decoy.

So with blurred vision and a banging headache, Davis stayed on the pitch and somehow managed to rush for 157 yards, catching two passes and becoming the first player in Super Bowl history to score three rushing touchdowns. That day he helped the Broncos win the Super Bowl 31-24 over the Green Bay Packers!

What's more, the blurry eyed Davis was named the game's MVP!

WHEN THE GOING GETS TOUGH...

Football is a tough sport to play. Day after day, and year after year, players put their bodies on the line for their teams, taking and making hit after hit.

It takes its toll on professional footballers, especially when they reach the latter stages of their careers.

In most cases, players know when the time is coming to hang up their cleats and retire. They'll discuss it with family, friends, teammates and coaches, before making their decision public and stepping away from the bright lights of pro football.

But one NFL player decided to retire in a totally different way.

30-year-old Vontae Davis had recently signed a $5 million contract with the Buffalo Bills and as far as anyone was aware, the former pro bowl corner still had a few years left of playing at the highest level.

But with recent injuries affecting him, and during a poor run of results for the Bills, Davis decided enough was enough and it was time to retire.

What was unique about Davis' retirement is that he didn't wait for the end of the season, in fact he didn't even wait until the end of the game!

With the Bills trailing the LA Chargers 28-6 at half-time, Davis walked off the pitch, into the locker room and out of the stadium! Davis had decided now was the time to retire, in the middle of an NFL game!

He was on his way home before any of his teammates even knew he had retired!

Davis later explained that he just felt he couldn't perform at the required standard anymore, and it had just hit him there and then that it was time to retire from the game he loved.

THE WRESTLING VIKING

WWE star Brock Lesnar has never been a dull man. He's been a multiple WWE champion, a wrestling champion in Japan and a World Heavyweight Champion in UFC.

But back in 2004, and at the height of his first stint in the WWE, Brock Lesnar, with three WWE championship belts in two years, decided he needed a change.

And so it was at the age of 27, that the 287 pound wrestling star set his sights on the NFL.

Lesnar hadn't played football since high school, but with his athletic ability, size, and fitness he wasn't short on offers to try out for a number of NFL teams.

The South Dakota native was keen on living out a boyhood dream of playing for the Minnesota Vikings and so that's where he headed.

Lesnar didn't end up making the cut and never went on to play an NFL game for the Vikings, instead returning to a successful career in the WWE via Japan and the UFC, but not before he had etched himself into Vikings folklore.

During a scrimmage in a try out game against the Kansas City Chiefs, Lesnar became enraged when a Chiefs player shoved one of his Vikings teammates hard in the back - he immediately went after the offending player, grabbed him and pulled out a wrestling style suplex move of him, much to the amazement of players on both sides.

This caused a huge brawl to break out - with Lesnar surely feeling more at home with the Royal Rumble he had just started than the actual football game itself!

DEFLATEGATE

Tom Brady is widely regarded as the greatest NFL player of all time, perhaps even the greatest sportsman of all time! Playing for 22 seasons and winning an amazing seven Super Bowls certainly backs up these claims.

Six of those Super Bowl victories came whilst playing for the New England Patriots, where quarterback Brady and no nonsense coach Bill Belichick created a winning mentality that would see the Patriots dominate the NFL.

There were plenty of ups and some downs during Brady's career, but there was perhaps no greater low point than the 2014 deflategate scandal that rocked the sporting world.

'Deflategate' as it came to be known, was an investigation into allegations that Brady and the New England Patriots broke NFL rules by purposely deflating footballs to gain an unfair advantage during an AFC title game against the Indianapolis Colts in the 2014-2015 season.

It was widely reported that 11 of the 12 footballs used in the first half of that game had less air in them than they should have had. Less air in the balls would mean they would travel differently when thrown and be different to handle when being caught.

An investigation found the Patriots to be at fault, and Brady, who was alleged to have known about it, was suspended for four games. The Patriots were handed a heavy fine and lost two draft picks as punishment.

Brady however, remained committed to his innocence and repeatedly denied all accusations.

And, with no direct evidence linking Brady to actually deflating the footballs, and no direct evidence that an advantage would even have been gained from doing so, the whole deflategate scandal could well have just been a lot of hot air about nothing!

It certainly didn't affect Brady's performances, as he went on to take the Patriots to another Super Bowl victory just a few months later after serving his suspension!

Health and safety is paramount in the modern game, from player welfare to the safety of equipment that the players use. But in 1960, things were a little different, leading to one of the most bizarre and dangerous stories the NFL has ever seen!

What started as a regular training session for the Green Bay Packers soon turned into a nightmare for one player in particular. Ray Nitschke, a linebacker in his third year of professional football, was part of a strong Packers defense and would go on to spend his entire career with Green Bay, winning 5 NFL championships as well as the first and second Super Bowls to be played.

But things could have been very different for Nitschke, who on on 31st August 1960, escaped near disaster due to a fortuitous change in the weather.

With the training session coming to a close, most of the Packers players had removed their helmets and shoulder pads, but as it started to rain Ray Nitschke picked up his helmet and put it on to stop his head from getting wet.

Moments later a 25 foot, 5,000 lb steel photographer's tower that overlooked the training field collapsed, crashing down onto the turf under a strong gust of wind, and landing on top of Ray Nitschke.

The helmet he had put on just moments earlier stopped a steel bolt from hitting his head and probably saved his life.

Pinned under the tower, Nitschke needed the help of all his Packers teammates to help him get out. Miraculously the only injuries he sustained were a twisted ankle and a battered helmet!

We doubt Ray Nitschke ever complained about it raining ever again!

FAN POWER

Every fan dreams of being able to help their team to victory with a crucial, match-winning play.

And in 1961 one Boston Patriots fan did just that!

The Dallas Texans and the Boston Patriots took to the field in an important AFL game with implications on who would make the playoffs that season.

As the clock ticked down to the end of the 4th quarter, Boston were ahead 28-21. Dallas had one last throw of the dice.

They were positioned just outside the end-zone, and a touchdown here would give them the chance to tie the game up at 28-28.

Dallas quarterback Cotton Davidson snapped the ball and threw to his open receiver in the end-zone.

But out of nowhere a hand went up to block the ball. The ball went dead and the game was over with Boston winning 28-21.

It wasn't until reviewing footage after the game that Dallas realized what had actually happened.

As Davidson had thrown the ball, a Boston fan had run out of the crowd into the end zone, putting his arms out just in time to affect the pass and win the game for his team - before disappearing into the crowd again!

Talk about taking one for the team!

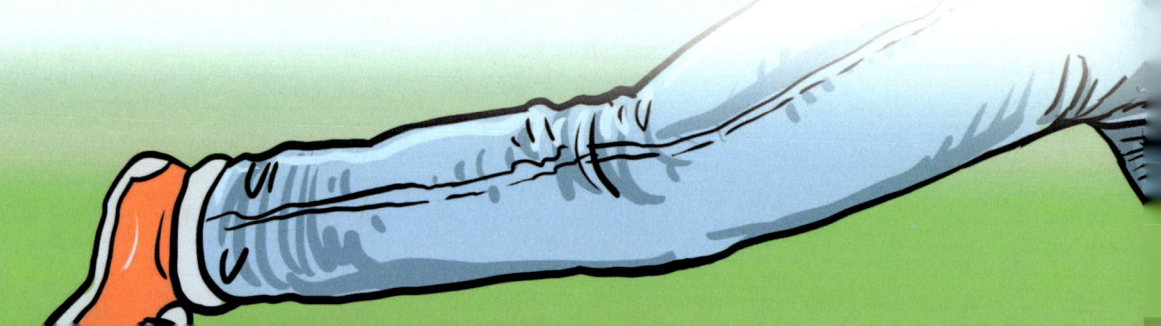

MAKING WAVES IN THE SUPER BOWL

Sarah Thomas loved sports. As a little girl in Mississippi, she played basketball with her brothers and dreamed of being a part of something big.

But Sarah didn't know yet that she was going to make history in football!

When Sarah was older, her brother invited her to a meeting for football referees. A referee's job is to make sure everyone follows the rules during the game.

Even though football was mostly for boys, Sarah decided to give it a try. She worked really hard and became the first woman to referee a big high school game in Mississippi. But Sarah didn't stop there!

Soon, Sarah was chosen to referee college football games, where she became the first woman to work in a college bowl game. Her skills were so good that the NFL noticed her. She was very excited about coming to the biggest football league in the world!

They invited Sarah to join a special program to train the best referees. In 2015, Sarah made history again by becoming the first full-time female referee in the NFL!

She wore her black and white stripes proudly as she stepped onto the field with the best players in the country. But her biggest moment came in 2021.

She was chosen to be the first woman to referee the Super Bowl—the most important football game of the year! As she walked onto the field, Sarah knew she was part of something special. She was showing girls everywhere that they can do anything, even if it seems impossible.

Sarah Thomas's journey proves that with hard work, big dreams, and courage, you can break barriers and make history, no matter who you are!

The Greatest Game

We've saved the best till last - with the greatest Super Bowl ever contested.

Anyone who follows football knew never to count out Tom Brady and the New England Patriots.

But what unfolded during Super Bowl LI is still impossible to believe.

In what many people believe to be the greatest game of football ever to have been played, a 39 year old Brady miraculously led his Patriots team from the brink of disaster to champions in the most incredible two quarters of football the Super Bowl has ever seen!

With the Atlanta Falcons holding a 25 point lead at the start of the third quarter, the Patriots looked down and out, and the Falcons were cruising to a famous Super Bowl victory.

But out of nowhere, the Patriots somehow managed to dig deep and started a fight back that will be remembered for decades to come.

25 unanswered points followed as the patriots found their rhythm with Tom Brady orchestrating the most unbelievable of comebacks.

19 of those points came in the 4th quarter forcing the game into overtime, where a shell-shocked Falcons team conceded another six unanswered points.

The Patriots had somehow done the seemingly impossible, and turned around a 25 point deficit to win the Super Bowl and get their hands on the Vince Lombardi trophy.

It was the Patriots 5th Super Bowl drawing them level on wins with Pittsburgh. It also gave head coach Bill Belichick a record five Super Bowl wins!

What's even more impressive is that at 39 years old, Brady was named MVP and thus cemented his name as *the* greatest of the game!

1. What unusual mistake did Jim Marshall make during a game in 1964?
a) He ran the ball into his own end zone.
b) He threw the ball to the wrong team.
c) He celebrated before scoring a touchdown.
d) He fumbled the ball on the goal line.

2. Kurt Warner once worked what job while waiting for his NFL opportunity?
a) Delivery driver
b) Grocery store shelf stacker
c) Taxi driver
d) Factory worker

3. How did Rocky Bleier overcome a significant obstacle to continue his NFL career?
a) He retrained as a kicker.
b) He underwent extensive rehabilitation after being wounded in Vietnam.
c) He switched teams to avoid military service.
d) He changed positions from running back to quarterback.

4. What was the controversy in the 1982 'Snowplow Game'?
a) The game was played despite heavy snow.
b) A snowplow cleared a spot specifically for a field goal attempt.
c) The game was postponed due to weather.
d) The opposing team's equipment was sabotaged.

5. What extraordinary act did Larry Izzo perform on the sideline during a game?
a) He made a game-saving tackle.
b) He went to the bathroom on the sideline.
c) He coached the team in a player's absence.
d) He caught a game-winning pass.

6. What tragic event preceded the New Orleans Saints' 2009 Super Bowl win?
a) Hurricane Katrina
b) An earthquake
c) A major fire in the city
d) A team plane crash

7. What did Jim Marshall do to survive a blizzard during a snowmobile expedition?
a) He built an igloo.
b) He used a flare gun to signal for help.
c) He burned his cash to keep warm.
d) He ate snow to stay hydrated.

8. What nickname was Thomas Henderson given due to his off-field behavior?
a) Fast Thomas
b) Hollywood
c) Wildcat
d) Maverick

9. Which two NFL teams combined to form the 'Steagles' during World War II?
a) Philadelphia Eagles and Pittsburgh Steelers
b) Chicago Bears and Green Bay Packers
c) New York Giants and New York Jets
d) Dallas Cowboys and Houston Texans

10. How many years passed before Norm Michael discovered he had been drafted by the NFL?
a) 10 years
b) 25 years
c) 55 years
d) 70 years

11. What is the 'Helmet Catch' famous for?
a) Winning the Super Bowl for the Giants
b) Being the first catch of the season
c) Being made with the player's helmet
d) Setting a record for longest pass

12. Why did Nate Burleson crash his car in 2010?
a) He was texting while driving.
b) He tried to save his pizza from falling off the seat.
c) He fell asleep at the wheel.
d) He was driving in heavy rain.

13. What infamous play is Mark Sanchez known for?
a) The Butt Fumble
b) The Helmet Catch
c) The Miracle Run
d) The Last-Minute Touchdown

14. Which fan managed to join the Steelers' locker room celebrations after Super Bowl XIII?
a) A young child
b) A security guard
c) An unidentified fan
d) A local reporter

15. Who was responsible for stealing Tom Brady's jersey after the 2017 Super Bowl?
a) A rival player
b) A news reporter
c) A Patriots coach
d) A fan

16. What is the 'Curse of Bobby Layne' associated with?
a) The Detroit Lions' lack of success
b) The Green Bay Packers' losing streak
c) The New York Jets' long playoff drought
d) The Dallas Cowboys' stadium curse

17. What unusual occurrence happened during Brett Favre's first NFL pass?
a) He threw it to himself.
b) He fumbled the ball before throwing.
c) He threw an interception.
d) He slipped and missed the throw.

18. How long is the waiting list for Green Bay Packers season tickets?
a) 10 years
b) 50 years
c) 100 years
d) Over 1,000 years

19. Which team accidentally contacted the wrong player during the 2011 NFL Draft?
a) New York Giants
b) Cleveland Browns
c) Miami Dolphins
d) Dallas Cowboys

20. Why did Eli Herring refuse to play in the NFL?
a) He had a career-ending injury.
b) He was drafted by the wrong team.
c) He didn't want to play on Sundays for religious reasons.
d) He wanted to play baseball instead.

21. Which famous actor was jokingly 'drafted' by the Atlanta Falcons in 1972?
a) Clint Eastwood
b) John Wayne
c) Marlon Brando
d) Paul Newman

22. How did Terrell Davis manage to play in Super Bowl XXXII despite severe migraines?
a) He took extra medication on the sideline.
b) He played as a decoy while nearly blind.
c) He skipped the game and rested.
d) He wore special sunglasses to reduce glare.

23. What did Vontae Davis do during a game that was highly unusual?
a) He scored a touchdown as a defensive player.
b) He retired from football at halftime.
c) He sacked the quarterback twice in one play.
d) He left the stadium without notifying anyone.

24. Which WWE star attempted to join the Minnesota Vikings in 2004?
a) John Cena
b) The Rock
c) Brock Lesnar
d) Stone Cold Steve Austin

25. What scandal involved Tom Brady and the New England Patriots in 2014?
a) SpyGate
b) DeflateGate
c) BountyGate
d) TapeGate

26. How did Ray Nitschke narrowly escape injury during a Green Bay Packers practice?
a) He avoided a lightning strike.
b) He put on his helmet just before a steel tower collapsed on him.
c) He jumped out of the way of a falling tree.
d) He dodged a car that drove onto the field.

27. How did a Boston Patriots fan help win a game in 1961?
a) He caught a pass from the quarterback.
b) He blocked a throw in the end zone.
c) He ran onto the field and tackled a player.
d) He distracted the opposing team's coach.

28. What happened in Super Bowl LI that made it so famous?
a) The game ended in a tie.
b) The Patriots came back from a 25-point deficit to win.
c) A player scored five touchdowns.
d) The game was postponed due to weather.

29. What dangerous mishap did happen during a Minnesota Vikings halftime show?
a) A hot air balloon broke free with a child inside.
b) A fireworks display went wrong.
c) A player was accidentally injured by a performer.
d) A snowstorm caused the stage to collapse.

30. What curse is said to have affected the Detroit Lions?
a) The Curse of the Bambino
b) The Curse of Bobby Layne
c) The Madden Curse
d) The SI Cover Jinx

1a, 2b, 3b, 4b, 5b, 6a, 7c, 8b, 9a, 10c, 11c, 12b, 13a, 14c, 15b, 16a, 17a, 18d, 19b, 20c, 21b, 22b, 23b, 24c, 25b, 26b, 27c, 28b, 29a, 30b.

101 FUN FACTS!

1. The NFL was founded in 1920 and originally called the American Professional Football Association.
2. A football is also called a "pigskin," but it's actually made from cowhide or rubber.
3. The Super Bowl is the biggest football game of the year and is watched by millions worldwide.
4. The Green Bay Packers are the only NFL team owned by their fans.
5. The Dallas Cowboys are known as "America's Team" because they have fans all over the country.
6. The Pittsburgh Steelers have won six Super Bowls, one of the highest in NFL history.
7. Each NFL game is divided into four quarters, each lasting 15 minutes.
8. A touchdown is worth 6 points, and teams can score extra points afterward.
9. The quarterback is the leader of the offense and throws most of the passes.
10. The Vince Lombardi Trophy is awarded to the Super Bowl winner.
11. NFL players wear helmets to protect their heads during the game.
12. The Chicago Bears have one of the oldest and most successful teams in NFL history.
13. The New England Patriots won three Super Bowls in just four years (2001-2004).
14. A field goal is worth 3 points and is scored by kicking the ball through the goalposts.
15. The NFL has 32 teams divided into two conferences: AFC and NFC.
16. The Super Bowl halftime show is famous for its music performances.
17. The NFL season has 17 regular-season games.
18. A football field is 100 yards long from end zone to end zone.
19. The first Super Bowl was played in 1967 between the Green Bay Packers and Kansas City Chiefs.
20. Tom Brady has won more Super Bowls (7) than any other player in NFL history.
21. The Detroit Lions play a special game every Thanksgiving Day.
22. NFL referees wear black and white stripes to stand out on the field.
23. The Miami Dolphins had a perfect season in 1972, winning every game, including the Super Bowl.
24. The NFL uses instant replay to review close plays and make sure the right call is made.
25. The Arizona Cardinals are the oldest continuously run professional football team.
26. Players who score a touchdown often celebrate with a dance called an "end zone celebration."
27. The Seattle Seahawks' fans are known as the "12th Man" because they're so loud they feel like an extra player.
28. The Heisman Trophy is awarded each year to the best college football player.
29. The Oakland Raiders were famous for their pirate-themed logo and tough image.
30. The Pro Bowl is the NFL's all-star game, featuring the best players from the season.
31. Wide receivers are the players who catch most of the passes from the quarterback.
32. A sack happens when the quarterback is tackled before he can throw the ball.
33. The NFL draft is when teams select new players from college to join their roster.
34. The Houston Texans are the newest NFL team, joining the league in 2002.
35. The Buffalo Bills went to four straight Super Bowls in the early 1990s but didn't win any.
36. Cheerleaders often perform on the sidelines to keep fans pumped up.

37. A safety scores 2 points and happens when the offensive team is tackled in their own end zone.
38. The Philadelphia Eagles' mascot is a bald eagle named "Swoop."
39. "Hail Mary" is a long pass thrown to the end zone in desperation at the end of a game.
40. The NFL logo has a shield with stars and footballs to represent the league's history.
41. NFL players often train year-round to stay in shape for the season.
42. The San Francisco 49ers are named after the 1849 Gold Rush in California.
43. The New York Giants are one of the oldest teams in the NFL, founded in 1925.
44. The Cleveland Browns are the only NFL team without a logo on their helmets.
45. The Tampa Bay Buccaneers have a pirate ship in their stadium that fires cannons when they score.
46. The Minnesota Vikings' fans perform a chant called the "Skol" chant to rally their team.
47. The Los Angeles Rams were the first NFL team to introduce a team logo on their helmets.
48. The Atlanta Falcons' mascot is a falcon named "Freddie Falcon."
49. The Kansas City Chiefs have a tradition of wearing all-red uniforms for big games.
50. The Chicago Bears' mascot is named "Staley Da Bear," after the team's original name, the Staleys.
51. The Denver Broncos' home stadium is one of the highest in elevation, making it harder to breathe.
52. The Indianapolis Colts have a famous horseshoe logo on their helmets.
53. The Washington Commanders' team name comes from the historical role of military leaders.
54. The Cincinnati Bengals' helmets have a tiger-stripe design to match their name.
55. The Baltimore Ravens are named after Edgar Allan Poe's famous poem, "The Raven."
56. A "fumble" occurs when a player drops the ball, and either team can recover it.
57. The New York Jets' fans are known for their loud "J-E-T-S, Jets, Jets, Jets!" chant.
58. The NFL Scouting Combine is an event where college players show off their skills for NFL scouts.
59. The New Orleans Saints' fans are called the "Who Dat Nation."
60. The Tennessee Titans' mascot is a superhero named "T-Rac."
61. The Super Bowl is usually played on the first Sunday in February.
62. The NFL has an official rulebook with hundreds of rules to keep the game fair.
63. The Jacksonville Jaguars' mascot is a jaguar named "Jaxson de Ville."
64. The Los Angeles Chargers were originally based in San Diego.
65. The Dallas Cowboys' cheerleaders are world-famous and have appeared on TV shows and in movies.
66. An interception happens when a defensive player catches a pass meant for an offensive player.
67. The Carolina Panthers' mascot is a black panther named "Sir Purr."
68. The Super Bowl winner is awarded championship rings to celebrate their victory.
69. The Las Vegas Raiders were originally known as the Oakland Raiders.
70. The Miami Dolphins' mascot is a dolphin named "T.D."
71. The New England Patriots' mascot is a revolutionary soldier named "Pat Patriot."
72. The Pittsburgh Steelers' logo has three colored diamonds representing steel.
73. The Arizona Cardinals' mascot is a cardinal named "Big Red."
74. The Chicago Bears' most famous player, Walter Payton, was nicknamed "Sweetness."
75. The NFL's official game ball is made by Wilson and is called "The Duke."
76. The Detroit Lions' mascot is a lion named "Roary."
77. The Seattle Seahawks have a tradition called the "12 Flag," which honors their fans.
78. The NFL regular season usually starts in early September.

78. The NFL regular season usually starts in early September.
79. The Green Bay Packers' fans are known as "Cheeseheads" because of the cheese industry in Wisconsin.
80. The Los Angeles Rams' mascot is a ram named "Rampage."
81. NFL players can run at speeds over 20 miles per hour.
82. The Buffalo Bills' mascot is a buffalo named "Billy Buffalo."
83. The San Francisco 49ers' mascot is a miner named "Sourdough Sam."
84. The NFL playoffs determine which teams will go to the Super Bowl.
85. The Kansas City Chiefs' mascot is a wolf named "KC Wolf."
86. The Cleveland Browns are named after their original coach, Paul Brown.
87. The NFL has a strict dress code, and players can be fined for breaking it.
88. The Tampa Bay Buccaneers' mascot is a pirate named "Captain Fear."
89. The Houston Texans' mascot is a bull named "Toro."
90. The Washington Commanders' mascot is a hog named "Major Tuddy."
91. The Cincinnati Bengals' mascot is a tiger named "Who Dey."
92. The Las Vegas Raiders' fans are known for their intense costumes and are called the "Black Hole."
93. The Carolina Panthers play in a stadium called Bank of America Stadium.
94. The Tennessee Titans' name comes from the powerful gods of Greek mythology.
95. The NFL has an annual Thanksgiving Day game, which is a big tradition.
96. The New York Giants' stadium is called MetLife Stadium.
97. The Atlanta Falcons play their home games at Mercedes-Benz Stadium.
98. The Denver Broncos' mascot is a live horse named "Thunder."
99. The Jacksonville Jaguars have a special section in their stadium called the "Bud Zone."
100. The Philadelphia Eagles' stadium is called Lincoln Financial Field.
101. The NFL's headquarters is located in New York City.

A QUICK FAVOR

Thank you for sharing this adventure with us! 📚✨

If you enjoyed the journey, we'd love to hear your thoughts.

Your reviews are incredibly important for my success!

Please leave a dash of kind words on your favorite platform. It really helps independent authors like myself!

Happy reading, and thank you for being a part of our story!

www.ingramcontent.com/pod-product-compliance
Lightning Source LLC
Chambersburg PA
CBRC091723070526
44585CB00008B/159